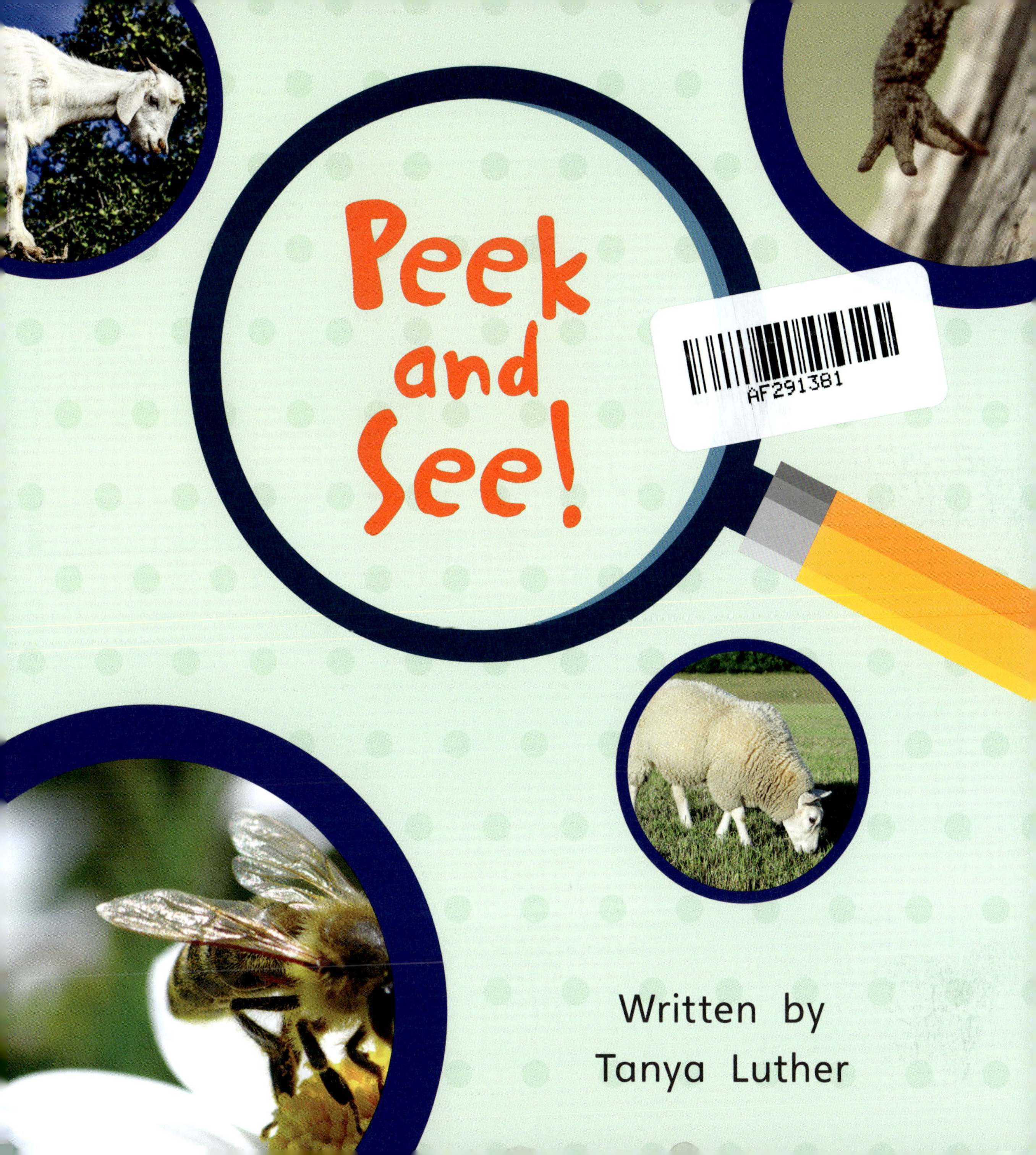

Peek
and
See!
Written by
Tanya Luther

Peek-a-boo! We can
spot the animals!

Peek-a-tail!

This is a goat.

Goats can kick
and run up hills.
They can go up high!

Peek-a-wool!

This is a sheep.

The sheep's wool is soft.
Its main food is grass.

Peek-a-wing!

This is a bee.

A bee has six legs.
It can buzz!
Queen bees are the biggest.

Peek-a-leg!

This is a toad.

Toads hunt at night.
They feed on slugs
and insects.

11

Peek and see!

a goat's tail

a sheep's wool

a bee's wing

a toad's leg